Fears, Doubts, Blues, and Pouts

Stories About Handling
Fear, Worry, Sadness, and Anger

H. Norman Wright and Gary J. Oliver

Illustrated by Sharon Dahl

CVP

Chariot Victor Publishing
A Division of Cook Communications

Chariot Victor Publishing
a division of Cook Communications, Colorado Springs, Colorado 80918
Cook Communications, Paris, Ontario
Kingsway Communications, Eastbourne, England

FEARS, DOUBTS, BLUES, AND POUTS
© 1999 by H. Norman Wright and Gary J. Oliver for text,
and Sharon Dahl for illustrations

First published as:
Ric & Rac's Woodland Adventure ©1995
HipHop and His Famous Face © 1995
Bruce Moose and the What-Ifs © 1996
Buford Bear's Bad News Blues © 1996

Printed in Mexico
03 02 01 00 99   5 4 3 2 1

This book belongs to:

_____

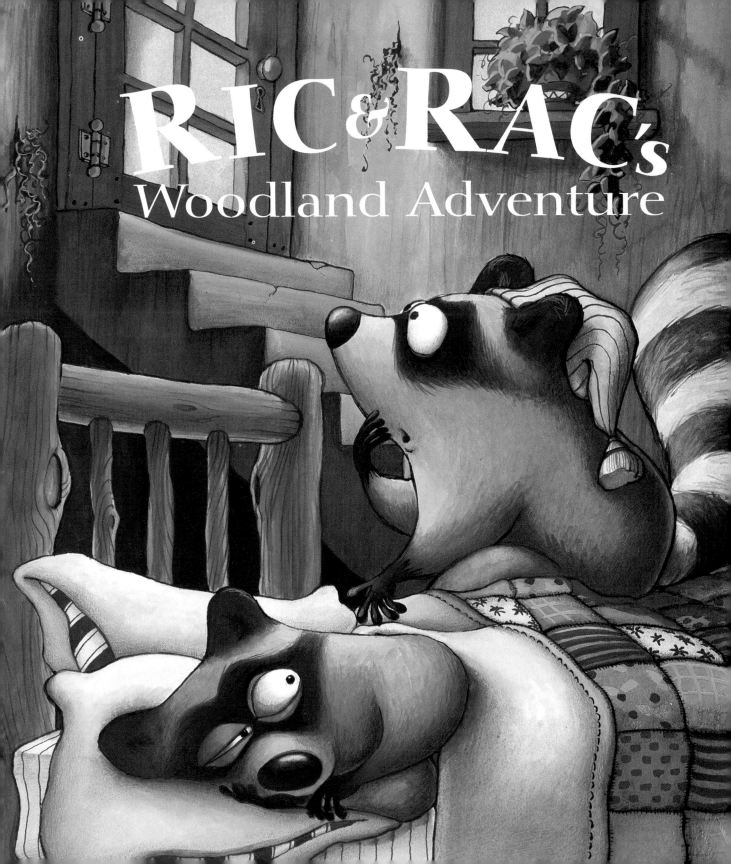

Ric woke up to the sound of scratchy noises and thumps outside the den he shared with his brother. Poking Rac, he whispered, "Wake up! I'm scared!"

"What's there to be scared of?" asked Rac, with a yawn.

Just then a dark shadow darkened their doorway. "That's what there is to be scared of," said Ric. He tried to hide behind his big brother.

Thump, thump, thump. The old tree above the den shook as bark fell off. The leaves shivered and the roots quivered. Ric dug his sharp nails into Rac's fur.

"Ouch!" said Rac. "Calm down. Remember that song we learned in Raccoon School?" He sang:
"*Fear can be a friend or fear can be a foe.*
That's something everyone needs to know."

Under his breath, Ric mumbled, "Ho, ho, ho." He didn't see how fear could be his friend. He didn't like to feel scared.

"Look!" said Rac, peeking out of the den. "It's only Buford Bear. He's hitting our tree to drive the bees away from their hive."

"**W**atch out," Ric said. "Those bees are mad and they could sting."

"Right, brother. Being a little afraid of bees makes us more careful. That kind of fear is our friend."

Just then Buford saw them. "My, my. Are you two coming out to help me get some honey?"

"Oh, no," said Ric. "Bees sting. They can hurt. Aren't you afraid of them?"

"Me, afraid? I'm big and strong. Why should I be afraid?"

"You mean you're never afraid, Buford?" asked Rac.

"Nope. Never."

"**B**oo!" said Ric, sneaking up from behind.

"Ah–h–h–o–o–o–w!" howled Buford.

Ric laughed. "See, I scared you!"

"No, a bee stung me," replied the bear. "O–w–w–w! Maybe I should have been more careful." And with that, Buford lumbered away.

"I don't believe Buford Bear," said Ric. "Isn't everybody afraid sometime, Rac?"

"**Y**es. But some—like Buford—don't want to admit they get scared. Others are afraid too much. They are scared of things they don't really need to worry about. That's when fear is a *foe*—getting in our way and making us unhappy." Rac thought a minute. "Ric, I'm going to take you to meet somebody like that. She lives on the far side of the woods. Are you afraid to come with me?"

"No!" said Ric. But his voice had a funny squeak in it. He had never been to the far side of the woods.

Through the forest the raccoon brothers went. They squeezed under fallen trees, swam across the stream, climbed over trees, and scrabbled through hollowed-out logs. Finally they came to the edge of the woods. But just as they stepped into the sunlight, a loud screech filled the air. Ric and Rac looked at each other, then raced back into the dark forest.

As soon as Rac found a hollow log, he jumped inside. Ric followed close behind. Safe inside, the little raccoon took a deep breath. "Pew!" he sputtered, "What's that awful smell?"

"Yuck!" said Rac, holding his nose. "I can't stand it!"

"It doesn't bother me," said a new voice.

"Who's that?" asked Rac.

"Hey, boys! It's me!" The new voice echoed in the darkness.

Ric and Rac looked through a knothole in the log and saw two yellow eyes.

"Who—are you?" asked Rac, his voice trembling.

The two eyes blinked. "It's me. Boo!"

The startled raccoons jumped out of the log and ran into the maze of trees. They quickly lost each other, scrambling in opposite directions to get away from those scary eyes.

"**R**ic!" called Rac.

"Rac!" called Ric.

Suddenly Ric realized he was alone in the woods.

Suddenly Rac realized he was alone in the woods.

Then Rac started to sing loudly, *"Fear can be a friend or fear can be a foe. It's something everyone needs to know."*

Ric heard the song, faintly at first. Then he sang an answer as loud as he could, *"Fear can be a friend or fear can be a foe."*

As the brothers listened and sang, they found each other at last—right back at the log where they started. They looked around for those scary, yellow eyes.

Suddenly, out of the log popped Smelly the Skunk. "Hi, guys! Boy, did I scare you. Ha, ha!"

"Ah–h–h–h, we knew it was you all the time," said Rac.

"Sure," said Smelly. "Well, I'm going back to smell . . . I mean *sleep*. Drop in again sometime."

"Rac, you were just as scared as I was, weren't you?"

"Yes. But that kind of fear wasn't good. If we had stopped and looked, we would have seen it was only Smelly."

"Well, when we ran from the screech before, at the edge of the woods, was that an all-right kind of fear?" asked Ric.

"I think so. It was an eagle, and they like to eat little raccoons like us. So our fear helped us look for safety. And now little brother, let's get back to the edge of the woods. I still want you to meet somebody."

Back through the woods they went. Finally, in a towering tree, they found a jittery looking creature who never stopped moving.

"Excuse us, Shirl Squirrel."

"Oh! You surprised me! What is it? I'm busy you know. I'm always busy."

"We have a question. Are you ever afraid?"

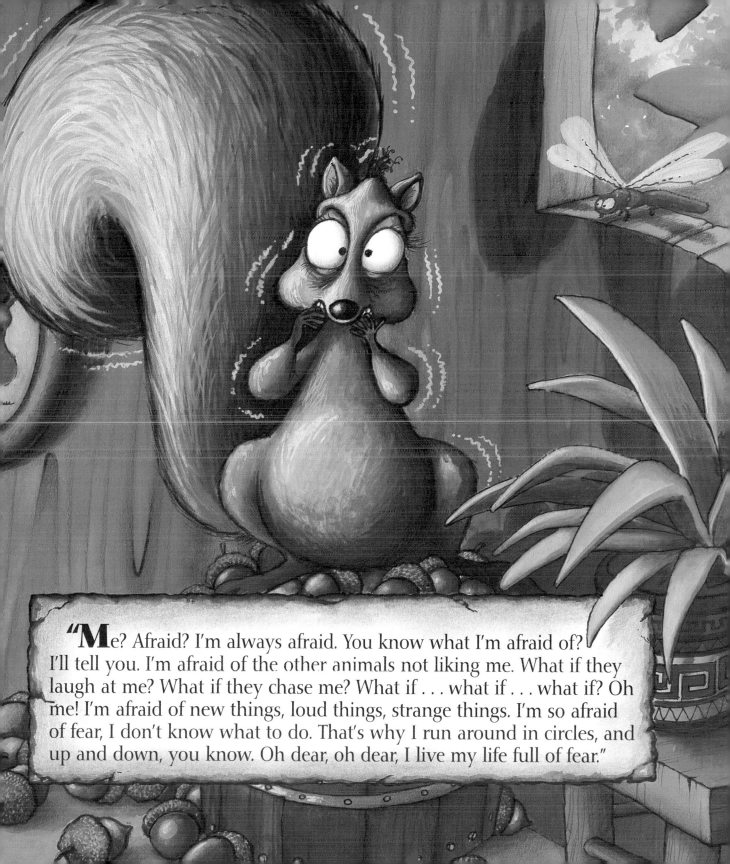

"**M**e? Afraid? I'm always afraid. You know what I'm afraid of? I'll tell you. I'm afraid of the other animals not liking me. What if they laugh at me? What if they chase me? What if . . . what if . . . what if? Oh me! I'm afraid of new things, loud things, strange things. I'm so afraid of fear, I don't know what to do. That's why I run around in circles, and up and down, you know. Oh dear, oh dear, I live my life full of fear."

Ric and Rac looked at each other and crept away while Shirl was still talking.

"She lives with all those fears. That's no fun," Ric said.

"Right. Those aren't friendly fears. She doesn't have any real reason to be so afraid all the time. Many of her fears are in her own imagination. If she would stop and think, or ask questions, she wouldn't be so afraid."

"But some fears are good, right?"

"Uh huh. If there's danger and you feel scared, that's good—because it keeps you from getting hurt. That's when fear is our friend."

Just then Ric heard a loud growl. He jumped!

But then he held himself very still and listened.
When he heard the growl again, he laughed. It was his
stomach, telling him it was time to go home for supper!

The raccoon brothers made their way through the forest again.

After a big supper of water snails, crayfish, and mushrooms, Ric lay
down for a long day's rest. Suddenly he woke to the sound of loud
scratching back and forth, right by the doorway of the den.

"Oh, no!" he thought. "Maybe something is trying to get through our
door! Or maybe a human is sawing down our tree."

Ric's heart started to beat faster and his paws got sweaty. His eyes
grew bigger, his tummy turned over, and he started to think. "What if . . .
what if. . . ."

He suddenly slapped his paw loudly on the ground and told himself,
"Stop that!"

He made such a noise that Rac woke up sputtering, "What's that?
What's happening?"

Ric took a deep breath, then bravely walked to the door. *"Fear can be a friend, or fear can be a foe. It's something I'm finally starting to know."* He sang the little song quietly to himself. As he walked, he felt less afraid. His heart didn't beat as fast and his tummy felt calmer.

He poked his head out the door and what did he see? Elwood Elk— shining his antlers on the side of the tree.

Elwood stopped when he saw Ric and said, "Oh, please excuse me." He turned away, looking very proper and proud.

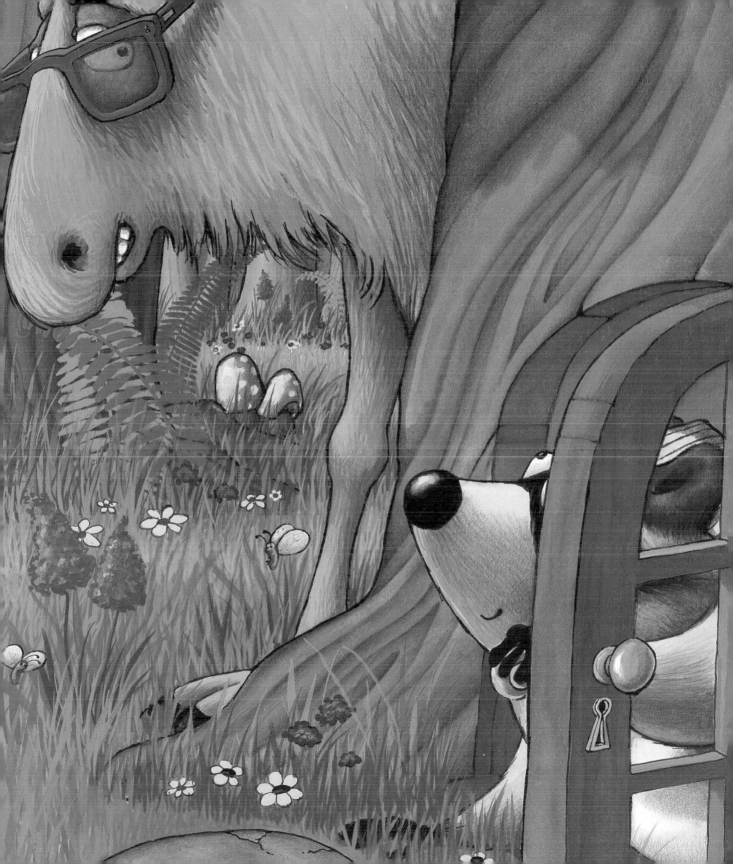

Ric smiled, sighed, and settled back inside his den. He told his brother, "Go back to sleep, Rac. It's nothing to be scared of. I found out what the noise was and took care of it. Isn't it great that we don't have to be afraid of every little thing?"

And with that he snuggled down and fell into a deep sleep.

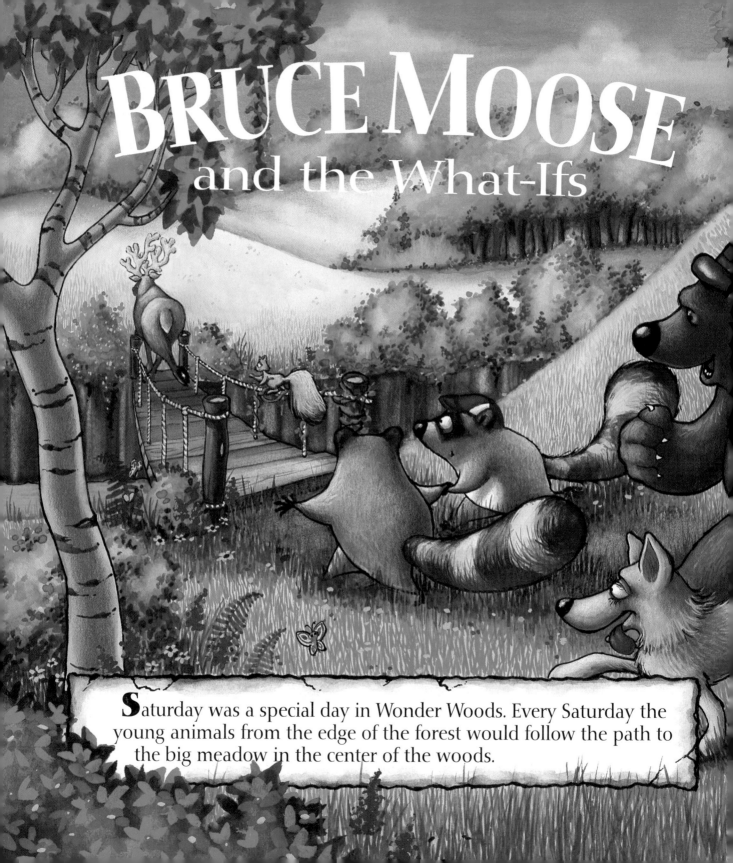

BRUCE MOOSE
and the What-Ifs

Saturday was a special day in Wonder Woods. Every Saturday the young animals from the edge of the forest would follow the path to the big meadow in the center of the woods.

They hopped and skipped and skittered along the path, sliding down the grassy banks, crossing over the bridge, and running into the meadow with great excitement. All along the path the friends would gather, laughing and singing their Saturday song:
   "It's Saturday! What do you say?
       Let's go to the meadow and play all day!"

One sunny Saturday, Buford Bear crawled out of his den and lumbered down the path. When he passed the oak tree, Ric and Rac scampered out to join him. Soon HipHop Bunny appeared, along with Elwood Elk—who brought Norman Nightcrawler along for the ride. At the gnarly, old, elm tree Brenda Blue Jay joined in. Then, out of nowhere, Shirl Squirrel zipped past, racing circles around all her friends.

But when the happy group at last came to the point in the road which was next to the pond near the trees where Bruce Moose lived, he was nowhere to be seen.

Buford turned to the others and said, "Bruce must have overslept today—just like last Saturday." The big bear began to bellow. "C'mon, slowpoke, wake up! It's time to go to the meadow to play!"

Nearby branches began moving slowly, and soon a pair of antlers emerged. A weak voice called out, "Sorry guys, I can't play today. I'm tired. And I don't feel very well."

The forest friends looked at each other, puzzled. "That doesn't sound like our Bruce Moose," said Elwood. "He used to love going down to the meadow."

"Right," exclaimed Shirl. "But this is the third Saturday in a row that Bruce has made some excuse not to play with us. Something must be wrong."

HipHop jumped in. "Maybe if I make one of my famous funny faces for Bruce, he'll forget what's bothering him and come out to play."

"Bruce," called Shirl. "You haven't come to the big meadow for the last three Saturdays. We don't think you're really sick. And you can't be that tired. What's wrong? Why don't you want to play with us?"

Finally Bruce stuck his head out of the bushes and sighed. "If I come out and play, something might happen," he said mournfully.

"Yeah," answered Norman, "we might have fun!" Norman laughed at his joke, but Bruce didn't join him.

"I meant that something bad might happen," Bruce said.

"Like what?" asked Brenda.

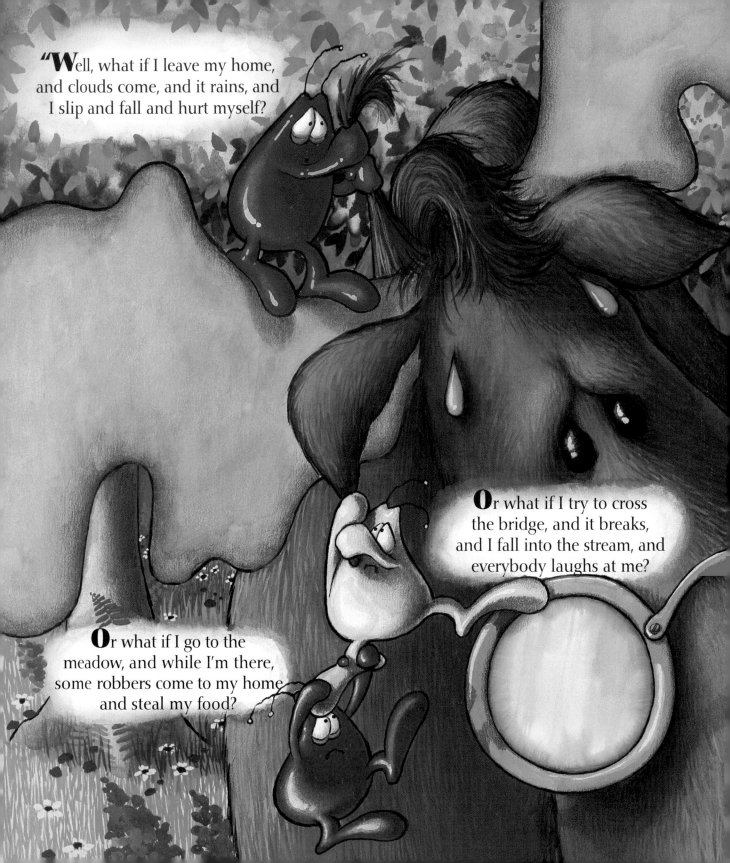

Before Bruce could name another What-If, Brenda Blue Jay blurted out, "I know what's wrong with Bruce!"

She flew to a little branch next to Bruce's worried face, looked straight into his big, brown moose eyes, and said, "You've got a serious case of the What-Ifs. You're letting those little guys boss you around and tell you what to do."

"What's a What-If?" asked Bruce.

Brenda explained, "A What-If is a tiny, imaginary creature, that makes you think of all the bad things that might happen if you do something. Sometimes it's called worry. Everybody has What-Ifs. But most of the time they stay little and harmless. If you listen to your What-Ifs, though, they get stronger and heavier."

Bruce Moose shook his head in wonder. His What-Ifs clung tightly to his antlers.

"If you listen to the What-Ifs long enough, you'll be too scared to do anything at all. They'll make your head hurt, upset your stomach, ruin your sleep, and take away your energy. You'll just stay at home and worry about all the terrible, awful, horrible things that might happen," said Brenda.

"**I** had that problem once," said Norman. "In those days, my nickname was Worry Worm. I worried that it might rain hard and flood my wormhole. I worried that I'd be out for a midnight crawl and a bigger animal would squish me. I worried that I'd fall into the stream right when a hungry fish came swimming by."

"What did you do?" Bruce asked.

"I didn't come out of my hole for a week. I worried about everything. I felt lower than slug slime." Then Norman stood up as straight and tall as a nightcrawler can stand and said, "Finally, I made up my mind I would not let those What–Ifs boss me around. So I told them to get lost."

"I didn't know you could do that," Bruce replied. "I thought those What–Ifs were right."

"Of course they're not right, you goofy moose," said Shirl matter-of-factly. "What–Ifs don't like the truth. They are cowards. If you tell them the truth, talk to your friends, and go ahead with your plans, the What–Ifs will go away."

"Yeah," said Norman. "They don't know what's going to happen. They just want to keep you stuck in your hole and stop you from having fun."

Elwood hadn't said anything for a while. Finally, in his mellow elk voice, he asked, "Bruce, has hiding in the woods made you feel better? Are you happier? Have the What–Ifs gone away? Or are there more of them?"

Bruce thought and thought and thought. His friends were right. Hiding hadn't helped. It had only made him feel worse.

After a long pause, Shirl said kindly, "We can't fix this problem for you, Bruce. So we're going to the meadow. Just remember that we're your friends. And we really want to see you there later. You know you can do it."

Slowly, the animal friends headed down the path, leaving Bruce alone with his What-Ifs. His head felt heavy with all the thoughts he needed to think. And the What-Ifs seemed to weigh a ton.

He glanced up and saw a What-If staring him in the eyes. Why not follow his friends' advice? he wondered.

"Listen you," Bruce said sternly. "Go away."

The What-If held on more tightly to Bruce's antler and made a nasty-looking face.

Bruce tried to remember what Shirl had said. Yell at the What-Ifs? No. Beat them off with a stick? No. Tell them the truth? Was that it? Yes!

"**H**ey! The truth is I'm going to leave my home and it won't rain. It's a beautiful, sunny Saturday," said Bruce, sounding more sure than he felt. Suddenly, with a *pop*, the What–If disappeared.

"And you up there," said Bruce, carefully walking down the path, "no one will come to my place and rob me while I'm gone."

He heard another pop and his head felt a bit lighter. "And my parents would *never* leave me alone. And my friends *will* play with me at the meadow."

Pop!

Pop!

It's working, thought Bruce

When he got to the bridge by the meadow stream, Bruce had only one What-If left. It didn't want to let him go. He thought he could hear it whispering in his ear, "You'll never get across that bridge; it's going to break. Give up. Go home."

But instead of listening, Bruce said in his deepest moose voice, "You're just plain wrong. I cross that bridge all the time, and I will again today." As the last What-If disappeared, Bruce lifted his head proudly and marched over the bridge and into the meadow where his friends were waiting for him.

All day he stayed and played tag, hide-and-go-seek, and his very favorite game, Duck Duck Moose.

Though the What-Ifs tried to bother Bruce a few more times, he only had to tell them the truth to make them disappear.

And that Saturday and all the Saturdays to follow were once again Bruce's favorite day of all in Wonder Woods.

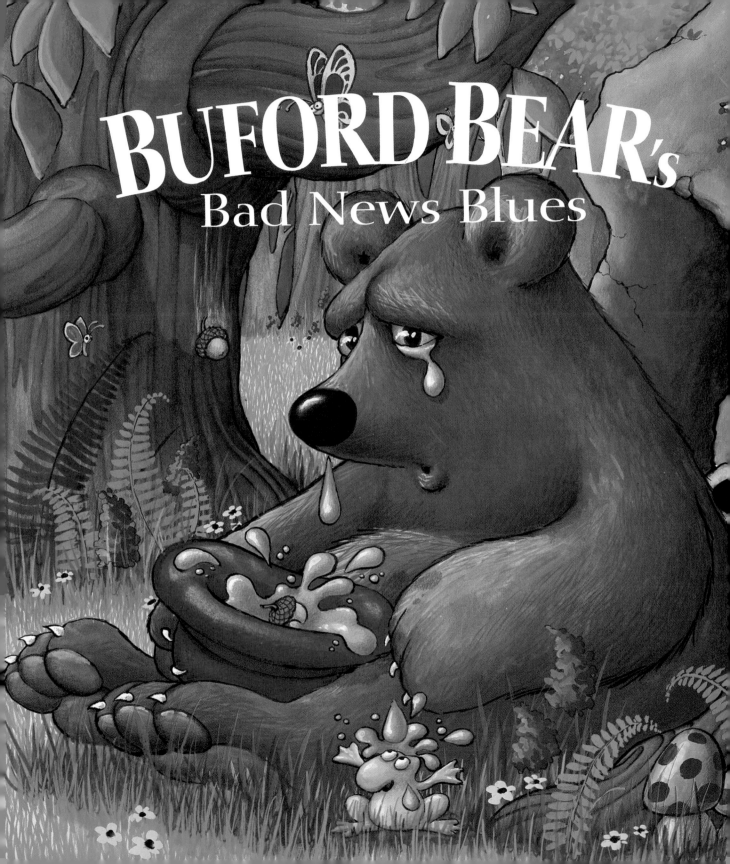

BUFORD BEAR's
Bad News Blues

A big, wet ball of water fell through the air. It landed in Buford Bear's bowler hat, along with the other tears which had dripped from his sad eyes.

Buford sat outside his den and sighed, "Oh me, oh my. I'm so sad. I wish I felt glad instead of so . . . bad!" Another tear fell with a splish and a splash.

Suddenly there was a bigger splash, and Buford was surprised to find a nut floating in his bowler. He looked up into the trees just in time to see Shirl Squirrel bouncing from limb to limb.

"Sorry about that!" said Shirl. "Am I bothering you?" She bounded down from one branch to the next, then jumped the last three feet to the ground. "What's wrong, Buford Bear?"

The grass behind Buford rustled, and a pair of pink ears belonging to Hip Hop Bunny were soon followed by the rabbit's worried face. "Yeah. I heard you sniffling and snuffling. Why the tears, big buddy?"

With a sniffle and a snuffle, and two more tears for good measure, Buford moaned, "Oh, woe is me. I'm just so sad. I wish I felt glad. But I feel so bad."

Shirl and Hip Hop looked at each other with surprise, then turned toward their friend.

"What's there to be sad about?" asked Shirl. "It's a pretty day. Look at all the grass and flowers to eat, the butterflies to chase, the hollow logs to crawl through."

"I don't care about those things," said Buford, with more sniffles than ever. "Anyway, the last time I tried to crawl through a hollow log, I got stuck."

Before Hip Hop could laugh at the idea of Buford stuck in a log, Buford shot him a mournful look. "And it's not funny, bunny. Nothing's funny anymore."

"**B**uford," Shirl said. "Let us help you. You've got a bad case of the blues and you need to talk to your friends. What's your problem, exactly?"

Buford said sadly, "Everything has gone wrong lately. And today doesn't look any brighter. No one understands. Maybe I'll feel this way forever and ever." Buford dumped out the tears from his soggy hat and plopped it back on his head.

"And don't even try to cheer me up," he added. "It won't help!"

"Don't you want to talk?" asked Hip Hop.

"I've been talking to somebody about my troubles," said the big bear.

"Who?" asked Shirl.

"Me, that's who," Buford replied.

"That's just the problem," said Hip Hop. "It's like one sad person talking to another sad person. It just makes you feel worse. Try talking to us now, okay?"

"Okay," said Buford with a very deep sigh. "It all started a few days ago when I was on my way to the pond. I passed Elwood Elk and Bruce Moose along the path, but they just ignored me. And Oscar and Oliver Otter just ran the other way when they saw me coming. I try to be friendly, but I think the other animals must not like me very much. Anyway, after that I decided to go on home to my den."

"Buford, we're your friends," said Shirl. "We think you're great! And the other woodland animals do too. They probably just didn't see you."

"Well, it doesn't feel that way to me right now."

"So what did you do next?" asked Hip Hop.

Buford sighed, remembering, "The next day it rained and rained, so I stayed inside my den all day long."

"Did you tell anyone else you were sad? Did you ask anyone to come over for a visit?" asked Shirl.

"No," said Buford.

"You mean you just moped around your dark, crowded, smelly den?"

"Maybe it's not the most cheerful place in the forest, but it is my home," said Buford with only a little hurt pride. "No, I didn't tell anyone my troubles. And I felt sadder and sadder to think that I was all alone. Then the really bad thing happened."

"What was that?" asked Hip Hop with concern.

Tears started to overflow from Buford's eyes again as he remembered. "The next day I felt a little better, so I decided to go across the woods to see my very best bear friend—Beulah Bear. When I got to her den, an old owl told me she had moved away, to the other side of the mountain. I don't think I'll ever see her again."

Hip Hop's face fell. "You know, my best bunny friend, Rad Rabbit, moved away last summer. I walked around with a sad face for the longest time. I didn't feel like doing much either."

"You mean it's normal to feel sad when you lose a friend?" asked Buford.

"Sure, it's normal," said Hip Hop, giving the bear a pat on his big brown paw.

"Oh my, Buford Bear," said Shirl, wringing out her tail which was now wet with the bear's big tears, "you do have a bad case of the blues. No wonder!"

"Just wait," said Buford. "It gets worse."

"After I found out about Beulah, I felt so low, I decided to visit my favorite berry patch. Nothing cheers me up like a mouthful of wild blueberries. So I hiked back across the woods to my secret spot. And it was gone! I guess the lightning from the storm a few days ago hit a nearby tree. The fire from the tree also burned up my berries!"

Buford sighed a deep sigh and rested his head in his hands. "This hasn't been my week," he said. "When I think about those lost berries, I get even sadder than before."

"Everyone is sad when they lose something that was important to them," said Shirl gently. "I lost my nest and half a tree full of nuts when lightning hit my last home. Sure, I was glad to get out safely, but I cried and cried about all my nice things and hard work—gone up in smoke. Losing things can be very hard. But it got better in time."

"So time can help? That's good to know," said Buford. "And talking with you has made me feel better. What else can I do?"

"I know," said Shirl, "let's all think about what we can do to help get rid of Buford's blues. You too, bear. Now that you've stopped crying, you can help make a plan."

The animals decided to think about their ideas in private.

Shirl whisked to the top of the tallest tree around and munched on a pine cone while she thought. "I've got it!" she said, finally.

Hip Hop burrowed into the grass, nibbling on some sweet clover nearby. "That's it!" he shouted after a while.

Buford stretched out in the warm sun, chewing on the honeycomb he'd saved for a special day. As he relaxed, he felt some of his sadness drain away. Suddenly, he sat straight up, saying, "Yes, yes, yes! Just the thing for my bad news blues!"

At the same time, the three animals met together by Buford's den.

"Listen to this," said Buford with excitement. "Why don't you two come hunting with me. Together we'll find a new berry patch, and share what we have with everybody."

"It'll be a party. A very bear-y blueberry party!" said Shirl, her tail twitching at the thought. "That's just what I was thinking of."

"Hey, you guys," said Hip Hop. "You stole my idea. It is a good one, isn't it? Blueberries to beat the blues."

"Say, why don't you ride up here with me?" invited Buford. So the three friends set off together.

Just then a butterfly landed itself squarely on Buford Bear's nose. His friends laughed out loud at the sight. And Buford suddenly found himself doing something he hadn't done for days.
He smiled.

Everybody knew that HipHop was a funny bunny—the funniest in the forest. And he wanted to stay the funniest. Each day he practiced his funny faces by the pond: wiggling his ears, bugging out his eyes, puffing his cheeks. He made silly faces. Wild and crazy faces. Wacky faces. HipHop's famous funny faces made his friends smile and laugh.

Except for one face that he just couldn't stop—even when he wanted to. When HipHop got really angry, his face wasn't funny anymore. Sometimes HipHop's angry face would even scare his friends away.

One lovely spring day HipHop went looking for his friends. He hoped that no matter what happened, he would be able to keep his angry face hidden away. He wanted his friends to like him, and not be scared off by his anger.

As he hopped down the tree-lined path, he saw his friends Carla Coyote, Elwood Elk, and Bruce Moose standing in the meadow. "Good morning," HipHop said in a cheery voice. "What are you doing?"

Carla answered, "This morning we can't decide what we want to do."

"Do you want to chase butterflies with me?" HipHop asked.

"Chase butterflies?" asked Elwood. "You've got to be kidding. I'm no good at chasing butterflies."

HipHop felt frustrated, but he didn't want his friends to know. So he stuffed his anger inside. But he could still feel it. And when he did this, his eyes got all squinty.

"**W**hat about hide and seek," suggested HipHop.
"I hate that game," complained Bruce. "I always lose."

This time HipHop stomped his foot in anger, but he didn't tell
Bruce what he was feeling. And now not only were his eyes still
squinty, but the insides of his ears suddenly turned bright red.

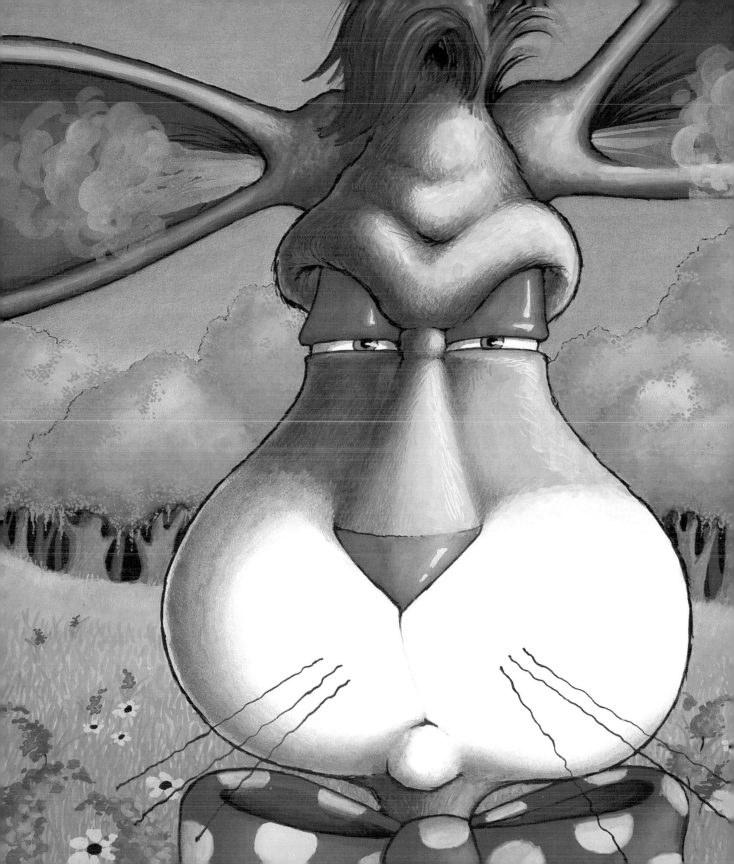

Finally, with a pouty kind of voice, HipHop said, "How about all of us racing to the pond?"

No one was surprised when Carla Coyote said, "Let's go!"

Off they ran just as fast as their paws and hooves would take them. Up the hill, across another meadow, and down the shortcut through the trees. And who got there first? Carla Coyote, of course.

When HipHop saw that Carla had beaten him, he got very, very angry. His eyes were still squinty; his ears were bright red. Next, his hair stood on end. In a loud voice he snapped, "You guys are no fun and I don't want to play with you any more!"

Bruce Moose replied, "HipHop, you're our friend. And you are the funniest bunny in the forest. But when you stuff and stomp and snap, you change. And then we don't like to be with you."

With that, Bruce and Elwood and Carla walked away.

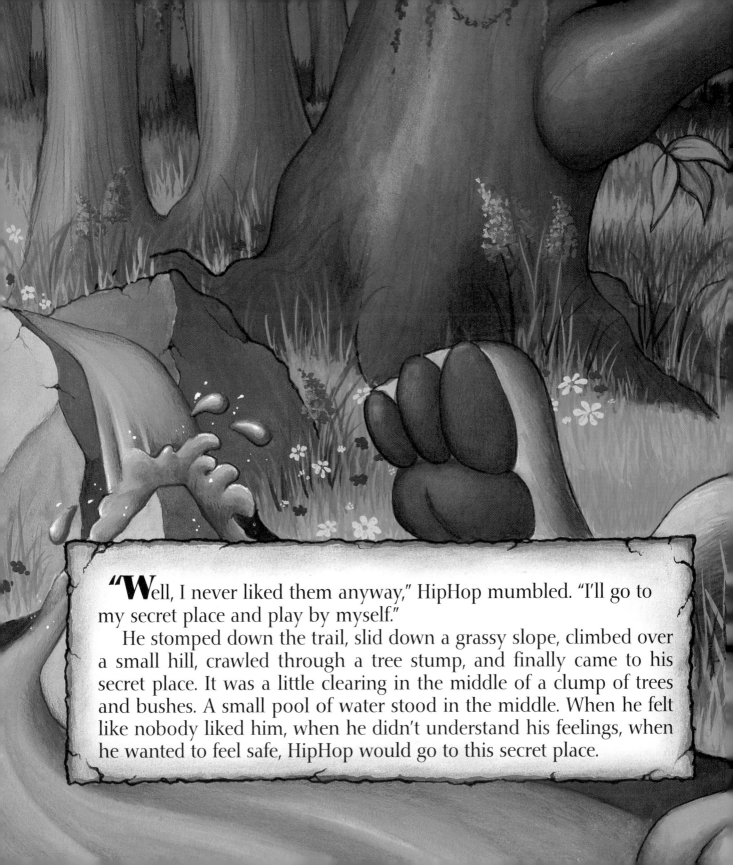

"Well, I never liked them anyway," HipHop mumbled. "I'll go to my secret place and play by myself."

He stomped down the trail, slid down a grassy slope, climbed over a small hill, crawled through a tree stump, and finally came to his secret place. It was a little clearing in the middle of a clump of trees and bushes. A small pool of water stood in the middle. When he felt like nobody liked him, when he didn't understand his feelings, when he wanted to feel safe, HipHop would go to this secret place.

HipHop sat down next to the little pool. He thought to himself, "Nobody will be able to find me here." So he sat and he sat. There was no one to make him frustrated, or hurt, or sad. But there was nobody to talk to either. He thought he would feel better, but he didn't. He felt lonely.

Suddenly he heard a funny noise. He looked around, but he didn't see anyone.

He heard the noise again.

He looked up just in time to see Brenda Blue Jay land next to him.

"Is that you, HipHop? You looked so different, I almost didn't recognize you," she said.

"What do you mean—different?" he asked gruffly.

"Well, take a look at yourself," said Brenda.

HipHop checked his reflection in the pool. No wonder Brenda didn't recognize him! Instead of the funniest bunny in the forest, he had become the ugliest bunny. His eyes were squinty, his ears were red, and his hair stood on end. As soon as he saw his reflection, his angry face became a very sad face.

"What are you doing here alone?" Brenda asked.

"Just having fun by myself."

"If you're having so much fun, why do you look and sound so sad?"

"I'm angry and I want to be alone," HipHop replied.

Brenda looked deep into HipHop's sad eyes and said, "Sometimes when we get hurt or feel frustrated, we get angry. And sometimes if we sit on our anger, it can become red hot. And when we let our anger get red hot, we can do or say things that hurt people."

"What do you do when you feel red-hot anger?" asked HipHop.

"My feelings don't get red hot very often."

HipHop was surprised to hear Brenda say that. He thought everyone felt things the same way he did. "Why don't your feelings get red hot very often?" he asked.

"Because," said Brenda, "when I start to get angry, I've learned to talk about what I'm feeling."

HipHop replied, "When I get angry, I stuff and stomp and snap."

Brenda began to clean her feathers. Then she asked, "Does it help to stuff and stomp and snap?"

"It doesn't," HipHop admitted.

"And how do you feel when your friends don't like you?"

"I feel hurt and sad. And then I feel mad."

"So, sometimes when you feel mad, it's because you first felt hurt and sad?" Brenda asked.

"I guess so," said HipHop. "I had never thought of that."

"Well," said Brenda—in that matter-of-fact way that Blue Jays sometimes have—"if stuffing, stomping, and snapping don't help, what else could you do that might work better?"

HipHop didn't know how to answer.

As Brenda started to fly away, she said, "Next time you want to stuff and stomp and snap, tell your friends what you feel, and see if that helps."

The next day, HipHop was on his way to the pond to chase butterflies when he saw his friends playing in the meadow. Elwood, Bruce, and Carla had been joined by Ric and Rac and Buford. He hopped over and hoped they would invite him to play. But they didn't. And it hurt. HipHop felt sad.

When Elwood saw that he was sad, and not mad, he said, "HipHop, would you like to play with us?"

"Sure," said HipHop. But as he ran over to join his friends, he tripped over a rock and rolled on the ground. When he got up, he could feel the mud sticking to his face. He heard his friends start to snicker. Then they laughed even louder.

HipHop was embarrassed that he had fallen in the mud. He didn't like his friends laughing at him. He felt his eyes getting squinty and his ears getting red. He knew what that meant!

"It's not funny," HipHop snapped. "It doesn't feel good to be laughed at!"

"We're not making fun of you," Bruce replied. "We just thought you were trying to be funny. You know, with one of your famous faces."

As soon as he saw his reflection in Elwood's sunglasses, HipHop realized how funny he looked. And he knew why everyone was laughing. HipHop started to laugh himself. "I guess I do look pretty funny." It felt good to laugh instead of stomping and snapping.

Then he tried out a few new funny faces. His friends laughed even louder, and even made some funny faces of their own. But everyone agreed that HipHop—with his famous face—was the funniest in the forest.

Faith Parenting Page

Ages: 4-7
Life Issue: My child doesn't always rely on God in the everyday situations of life.
Spiritual Building Block: Trust

Ric & Rac's Woodland Adventure

Visual Learning Style: Explain to your child that fear is a God-given emotion that everyone experiences. Talk with her about things it's wise to fear and things we don't have to be frightened about. For example, it's wise to fear lightning when we're outside because lightning is dangerous, and common sense tells us to seek safety. However, we're safe inside our homes or cars, so we need not fear. Draw a line down the middle of a poster board. On one side, have your child draw pictures of things she should fear, and on the other side, the things she doesn't have to fear.

Auditory Learning Style: Share what scared you when you were a child. Describe what you did to overcome your fears. Ask your child what her biggest fear is. Brainstorm specific things she can do when she's afraid.

Tactile Learning Style: Teach your child how to shoot "airplane prayers" to God. Airplane prayers are quick, silent prayers said in everyday situations. For example, on your child's way to school, she can "fly" up a prayer such as, "God, please help me do well in the music program today." For best results, help your child write down her prayer on a piece of paper, fold it up into a paper airplane, and throw the airplane into the air. Assure your child that God hears every prayer. As her prayers are answered, review how God answers each one (even if the answer is no).

Bruce Moose and the What-Ifs

Visual Learning Style: Discuss your child's definition of worry. Explain that God has given us the ability to care about people and things. But when we focus on the terrible things that might happen, our healthy caring can turn into worry. When worry controls us, it can have a bad effect on us and on those we love. Print Philippians 4:6 on a piece of paper and hang it in your child's room: "Do not worry about anything. But pray and ask God for everything you need. And when you pray, always give thanks" (NCV). Have your child cut out or draw pictures of things that worry him. Using a felt board, label one side "what-if" and the other "trust." Place the pictures on the what-if side of the board. Talk about all the what-ifs that go along with each picture, then pray through the Scripture verse and move the picture to the trust side of the felt board. When you pray through the verse, say this aloud with your child: "Do not worry about (the problem). But pray and ask God for (a specific prayer request). And when you pray, give thanks for (something your child can be thankful for concerning the what-if situation).

Auditory Learning Style: Ask: "What were some of Bruce's what-ifs and how were they affecting him? Do you ever worry about anything? Tell me about it." If you can, tell a story about a time you worried about something, then found out that your worries were unfounded.

Tactile Learning Style: If your child has some action figures or Lego people, help him set up some what-if situations. For example, if he worries about being laughed at while playing with other kids, use the figures to play through the situation with a few realistic solutions.

Buford Bear's Bad News Blues

Visual Learning Style: Talk together about things your child can do when sad or depressed. Encourage her to (1) talk about it, (2) express her feelings about it, (3) look at both the loss and the positive things in life, and (4) if there was a loss, help your child say good-bye to whatever she lost. Give your child a special scrapbook or journal she can use to express her feelings about her sadness or loss. Give her a few ideas about how to do that: put in photos and captions, draw pictures, paint, write stories or poems about her feelings, and so on.

Auditory Learning Style: Ask your child to give you her definition of sadness. Ask: "Do you think sadness is good or bad?" Explain that sadness is a God-given emotion that everyone experiences at times. Share what made you sad when you were a child. What was your biggest loss as a child? Describe what helped you overcome your sadness.

Tactile Learning Style: When your child experiences sadness, help her learn how to say good-bye to the things she has lost. Put the following items around the room and help your child see how each item can be used to express her feelings: a pillow (you can cry on it or punch it), paper and a pen (you can write down your feelings or write a letter to a person you're sad about), a phone (discuss who your child might call), and so on.

Tactile learning activity adapted from Fun, Change, Why Believe *by Linda Kondracki Sibley, David C. Cook Publishing.*

HipHop and His Famous Face

Visual Learning Style: Explain to your child that anger is a God-given emotion that all of us experience. There are different ways to express anger—some are helpful and some do harm. Discuss various healthy ways your child might handle his anger, and have him draw pictures of himself handling his anger in healthy ways. Ask: "What is good about the way you handle anger in this picture?" (I don't hurt other people, animals, or things.)

Auditory Learning Style: Ask your child: "What did HipHop learn from Brenda Blue Jay? (He learned that stuffing and stomping and snapping doesn't help. He learned that underneath his anger are other emotions. He learned that it is important to share what you are really feeling.) Share a couple of examples from your own life—one when you lost control and another when you handled your anger in a healthy way.

Tactile Learning Style: Look for a teachable moment—in this case, a time when your child is angry and not expressing his anger well. If you can, put the object your child is angry about on a table or somewhere in plain sight. (If you can't physically produce the object of your child's anger, write it down on a piece of paper.) Cover the object or paper with a blanket, then put the blanket in a box. Encourage your child to snap and stomp around as much as possible. Get down on the floor and play along with your child too! Then ask: "Did this help solve the problem?" Point out that your child's problem is still "in the box." Explain that stuffing, stomping, and snapping doesn't make anything better—it just makes it harder to get at the real problem. When your child is ready, take the blanket out of the box and wrap it around him. This can be a symbol that you want to create a safe place for him to discuss his true feelings with you—he can cry or be upset if he needs to. Help your child express his feelings. Now you have "uncovered" the real problem. If there's anything that can be done about the problem—for example, if a toy can be fixed or apologies made—now is the time to do it. If not, it may be enough just to help your child express his feelings.